Power Thoughts

Empowering For A Successful Life

Sylvia A. Hayes

Alive & Kickin Productions, LLC

Publisher

Power Thoughts

Empowering For A Successful Life

ISBN 978-1-7353858-0-8

Alive & Kickin Productions, LLC, Publisher

Printed by Lulu.com

Dedications

I dedicate this book to my sisters Carol Marshall and Martha Cole who are both teachers and is just as dedicated as I am to make a difference in the lives of children. Who believe that education is more than just English, math and science but being prepared to deal with the world with wisdom in the everyday activities of living. Thank you for sharing your words of wisdom with me. Much love to Akbar Imhotep, my friend forever, who encouraged me to finish this book which I started writing years ago. I also want to give a shout out to my English teacher at Utica Jr. College, Mrs. Rosa Crisler, whom I appreciate very much. I didn't know it at the time, but her English Composition class has really helped developed me into the writer that I am today. But most of all I want to give kudos to my students who were wide open to receiving my daily words of wisdom. Your enthusiasm in listening, willingness to share and your reports as to how the "Power Thoughts" has helped you in your daily lives has encouraged me to write this book and continue to help people stay or get on the right track in their lives. To you I am most grateful.

Love you much

About the Author

Sylvia Hayes was born and raised in Magee, Mississippi. After graduating from Magee High School she went to Utica Jr. College and then on to the University of Southern Mississippi. Her love for the arts and writing were discovered at a very early age. She also has a love for the medical field and teaches Health and Stress management. As a theater major and after moving to Atlanta, you can say that some of her accomplishments are being seen on the screen in movies such as "Night School", "Full Count", "The Cotillion", "The Gospel", and "Sunday Morning Rapture" just to name a few. Being a storyteller and a certified Toast Master gave her the courage to host the talk show "Good News @ PrimeTime" that she has been producing since 2001 on public access television. She is the co-owner of a production company which created and produces "The Church Ladies Cooking Show" as well as the producer and co-host of "Alive & Kickin" which is a health and wellness show.

As the parent of two children, she realized that not all children receive positive actions and affirmations from their parents and peers. "The children are our future", she would say. Realizing that her life will someday be in their hands, she got a job as a school bus driver and did the 'Power Thoughts' every morning before releasing them. Their grades went up, goals were set, behaviors were changed, friends were made, mindsets were changed, respect was present and there were no violence on her bus. This was done with the middle and high school students. She talked more to the children than their own parents and in which many expressed their gratitude.

Since she is no longer in the school system, she decided to put all her 'Power Thoughts' into a book to continue to enlighten and empower the future leaders as well as their parents and other adults for years to come.

Statements from the Students

These are statements written by my students through out the years from when I was driving the school bus. They are the reason that I wanted to continue to instill wisdom and knowledge into the future.

Your Power Thoughts in the mornings motivated me for the rest of the day. I feel more empowered and it helped me in school. **David R.**

Your Power Thoughts helped me and my friends when I shared them. I enjoyed them and feel that everyone should have them every day. **Mery M.**

You have talked to me more than my parents have. I feel that I am more ready for life. **Jon S.**

Your Power Thoughts taught me how to be smart and wise. It made me think about others when I am around them. **Oscar B.**

The Power Thoughts made me change the way that I think. It helped me a lot. **Joan S.**

I was helped by the Power Thoughts. It made me view things differently. It made me think about the way we treat others. **Anonymous**

Sometimes your Power Thoughts helps me with what I am going through. I think about what is best for me even when people disagree with my decision. It inspired me to stop procrastinating. **Jasmin V.**

The Power Thought gave me tips for when I get older and become someone in life. It made me communicate more with people and made me believe that dreams do come true and that anything is possible. **Anonymous**

The Power Thoughts helped me think about things from a different perspective and it started my day off better. It has motivated me to push to do my best no matter what. **D. Bibiano**

The Power Thoughts taught me to care and respect others. I now treat my family and friends better. **Bella**

I loved the Power Thoughts. It encouraged me to follow my dreams. I have been empowered to be a leader instead of a follower. **A. Servin**

The Power Thoughts helped me to make more friends. My self-esteem has risen and I feel happier. **Melody**

The Power Thoughts has helped me. Now when someone calls me a nerd I take it as if they are trying to say that I am smart. **Jesus V.**

I have been empowered by the Power Thoughts in knowing that I should be happy even if people try to bring me down. Thanks for giving us good advice on various things. **Andrea C.**

Words of Empowerment

1. You control your destiny. You have the power to succeed. Let no one discourage you from reaching your mightiest dream.

Whatever your goal in life is, go for it. People will try to discourage you from fulfilling your dreams simply because they can't see it as a possibility. They may tell you to quit dreaming and get a real job. Or you are not smart enough to do that. They may come right out and say you will never make it. But remember you are in control of your destiny and what happens to your life. Everyone else are onlookers.

2. If it is to be, then it is up to me.

Don't wait for someone to drop something in your lap for you to claim success. You've got to get out there and make it happen. You are as successful as you work. If you put a little into a project, you will get little in return. If you work very hard, then the rewards will be great.

3. Always believe in yourself whether anyone does or not.

It is up to you to believe in yourself. The mountain will

be hard to climb when people are throwing negative things at you. But if you believe in yourself and strive for your heart's desire, then success is yours.

4. Stand up for what you believe in but let it be the right thing.

People often back down from what they believe in because everyone else has another opinion – majority rules. In the case of a jury, if you think that the party is innocent and everybody thinks he's guilty, stand up for what you believe in. You might be right. I know the pressure will be great but sometimes you have to just stand up.

5. Know when to stand and when to sit.

Always being right isn't necessarily the best thing. Sometimes you need to just sit and listen.

6. Be quick to think and slow to speak.

Oftentimes when we are emotional we will say things out of anger or desperation. This is the wrong thing to do. You never want to say anything that will come back and haunt you later. For example: You are arguing with a person and you yell "I will kill you". Two days later they find him dead. Since several people heard what you said, where do you think they will start looking? Think about tomorrow's consequences for today's words before you say them.

7. Only a fool surrenders to dares.

Oftentimes a person will dare you to do something. Many times it is to do something wrong. If you surrender to the dare and get in trouble, they will be free and laughing at you. So whenever someone dares you to do something, tell them "only fools surrender dares."

8. Don't be afraid to ask for what you want.

Ask for whatever you want. You can only get a yes, no, maybe or a not now answer. Ask your boss for that raise or promotion if you think that you deserve it. Ask for a company picnic or free fries if you feel that you have been waiting too long for your food. Ask for a discount on an item in the store. If you don't ask for it you won't get it. People can't read minds and they are not always thinking on the same level as you are.

9. God Bless the child who's got his own.

Always strive for independency. Have your own car, food, clothes, roof, tools and supplies. You don't want to have to depend on anyone else for the things that you need or want. Having to wait on someone to take you to the store is no fun when you need medicine right now. Emergencies are ok but to constantly borrow from someone quickly wears out your welcome mat and resistance will come into play. Working to be self-sufficient gives you a sense of self pride and gratification as well as your sense of value will heighten.

10. It's not what you say but how you say it that gets you the results that you get.

Two people can make a statement using the exact same words and will receive 2 different reactions simply because of the deliverance of the statements. One could get a warm embrace while the other could receive a punch in the face.

11. Once you start on a task, don't stop until it's done.

People often start things and never complete it. Many lives are filled with unfinished business. They often give up or put it aside for one reason or another. The only way you are to accomplish anything is to finish the task.

12. Be it great or be it small, do it well or not at all.

Small tasks have great values. Don't discount any task because it is a small one. The smallest detail could save many lives or hours of time.

13. Our worst enemy is fear itself.

Fear has stopped many accomplishments. Fear of

asking for a raise. Fear of leadership promotions. Fear of being called a nerd. Fear of asking one out on a date. Fear of trying out for a sports team or any other organization. Fear of making new friends. For some reason, we are programmed to fear objections and rejections. We have power beyond measure and are afraid to access it. Step outside of that comfort zone and aim for the things that you want. That is the only way that you will excel. Conquer fear, don't let fear conquer you.

14. Be aware of the dog that brings you the bone.

When a person continues to bring bad news to tell you about who's talking about you or who was seen talking to your mate, you should start to think about why are they constantly bringing you that information? Do your own investigations before you react. You could be reacting to some false information that's given to you by your friend. There may be a motive to have them telling you this information which could cause a breakup or a bad relationship. On the other hand, they could have your interest at heart and want the best for you. They are telling you the information so that you can be aware of what's going on.

15. You are your brother's keeper.

If you know someone who doesn't have enough food to eat, share yours with them if you have extra. If you see someone who is being mistreated, speak up, especially if it's domestic abuse. Sometimes you can throw in a kind word to cool the fire. Don't say, "It's not my child" when you see that the child needs shoes. Sometimes the parents may not be able to afford them. Buy the child some shoes or pass down your child's small shoes. Don't make the child suffer. Remember, your trash is someone else's treasure. Donate to the homeless shelters instead of throwing items away. Always visit the sick and shut-in as well as the elders. It will bring a little sunshine into their lives and will make you happy as well. One day you may be in their shoes.

16. To make friends you must show yourself friendly.

Everyone doesn't have that 'assertive' personality. Sometimes people want to be your friend but they don't know how or are afraid to approach you. You will need to walk up to people and start a conversation. It can be as simple as talking about the weather, commenting on the food, or just asking a question. With 2 people being shy, someone has to make the first move. If you are walking, you can ask if they want to walk with you. Put forth an effort to make friends.

17. On your way up the ladder of success reach back and pull someone up with you.

Don't step on people when we are trying to reach your goal. Success in the first round is not guaranteed. When you share knowledge and treat people right on your way up the ladder of success, they will be there for you should you slip and start to fall. They will cushion your fall and pick you back up. If you were mean and nasty to people they will watch you fall and laugh at you.

18. Life is like a boomerang - whatever you throw out it comes back at you.

If you feed someone when they are hungry, someone will feed you when you are hungry or they may feed your child. If you gave someone a coat when they were cold, someone will provide for you in your time of need. If you tried to teach someone something, somewhere down the line someone will teach you something. If you were nice to a stranger in a new town, someone will be nice to you or they may be nice to your child when they are out of town. Whatever you throw out it will come back to you somewhere in the future. It may be 10, 15 or 30 years from now, but you will reap the benefits of your good deeds or your bad deeds. Remember life is like a boomerang, you will reap the benefits of getting an education, treating people right, doing your best on a job, and putting the right things into your body, just as you would reap the consequences when you rob, steal, cheat and beat.

19. Procrastination can cause you to lose your destination.

You never know what tomorrow holds for you. Don't put off doing a project when you can do it earlier. Your projected time may find you sick or too preoccupied to do it. Just because a company is taking job applications until Friday, doesn't mean that Friday is when they will choose the right candidate. They may spot him on Wednesday. Waiting until the last minute to study for a test can cause you a lot of stress and you may forget what you have read and therefore not passing the test. Waiting until the last minute to go to a business meeting could cause you to miss out. You could have a flat tire or get caught in a traffic jam and it made you 45 minutes late. You missed out on a great opportunity because the meeting was only an hour. Put procrastination on the back burner.

20. You are your parents 'Bragging Rights'; give them something to talk about.

Young and old parents love to brag about their children. They take the school day pictures to work to show off their kids. They brag about the touchdown that their sons made or their child making the cheerleading squad or homecoming queen. They brag about their achievements on the job. Parents are always so proud of their children. They love to show them off. Don't disappoint them.

21. Don't wait for the ship to sail in, swim out to it.

People often wait for things to happen before they make that next move. They say "I'm going to wait and earn a certain amount of money before I get married and have children". "I'm going to wait for the perfect

16

job before I do this". That perfect job may not ever happen. Go ahead and make things happen. Don't just wait for it to happen, you have to take action and make things happen.

22. Success is not always measured by how much money you make but how happy you are with what you are doing.

Believe it or not, a lot of rich people are unhappy. They worry about having true friends and people taking from them. If you love and honestly worked hard for the position that you are in, you can rejoice with pride. You may not be where others say that you should be but you are happy with where you are and you feel good about it. Meeting your financial obligations and being happy and at peace is more important than having an overabundance of money. Now, that is success.

23. Learn all you can, about everything you can.

Know who your city and state officials are. Learn how to cook a variety of dishes. If you drive a car, know how to change a flat and check the fluids in it. Why pay someone $25 to change a $7 filter when it only took 5 minutes to change and you can do it yourself? If you take medicines, know the side effects. Find out what causes your illness and how to fix it. Read the labels on your food so that you will know what you are putting into your body. Know your citizen's rights. Know what's going on in your community, heck, know your neighbors. Never stop learning. You are never too old to learn.

.

24. Never let anyone dictate to you how you should feel about yourself.

If you look in the mirror and say, "I look good" when you bought a dress that you just love, that feeling and thought is all that matters. No one has the same taste in clothing. So if the dress looks good to you, you're the one that counts. Always love yourself regardless as to what anyone else may say, because God doesn't make mistakes. Sometimes people will try to make you feel bad about yourself because they feel bad about themselves. Misery love company. In domestic abuse cases, the perpetrator would tell the victim, "you are ugly and no one wants you" and they are the only one who will take you. Don't believe that. They are trying to brainwash you into staying with them and have power over you. Don't you let that happen. You are a beautiful person and you know that. When you look in the mirror you can see that you are a beautiful person. Don't let anyone dictate to you how you should feel about yourself because you know that you are a beautiful person.

25. There are positive people and there are negative people. There are people who add to your life and there are people who take away from your life. Hang around the positive people and the

people who add to your life. Stay away from the negative people and people who take away from your life.

You will find that there are people who don't want to do anything with their lives. They talk negatively about things that you want to do or try to put down people who are doing good things in their lives. You don't want to be around people who are always getting into trouble and people who always put you down for trying to do something good or positive with your life. Those are the people who will keep you down. They will get into trouble and try to take you down with them. Stay away from those people. There are people who are eager to succeed in life. Those are the people you want to hang with because they want to do good and they will encourage you to do good as well.

26. Every dream has wings. You have the choice to either spread them and soar or clip them and lay dormant.

If you have a dream to work for the airlines and travel around the world go for it. Don't say that it will be too much work or they won't hire you. Don't be afraid to go after your dream and work hard for it. That is the only way that you will succeed. Hard work is the path to your success. If you only dream and don't put forth an effort to accomplish your goals, then you will only be dreaming.

27. Don't ever tell yourself 'no', let someone else do that.

If you see a job posted that you know that you can do but you don't meet all the qualifications that the employer has listed, go for it anyway. Don't say, "They won't hire me". Often the employer will list attributes to weed out the bad people. Don't say, "I don't qualify" if you know that you can do the job. If you want to do something different or special on your job, don't automatically say, "They won't let me". Let them tell you that you can't do it. If you want to buy a car with no down payment, don't say that they won't do it. Tell them what you want and let them tell you that they can't do it. Whatever you want ......ask for that job, ask for that discount and let them tell you no. Who knows, you might get a yes.

28. Your tongue is a powerful tool, use it wisely.

Saying the wrong thing to a child can scar and destroy him for the rest of his life. Sometimes people can say things that will cause them to lose their life or lose someone else's life. You can say things that can cause you to lose your job or cause you to gain a job. It can make friends and it can make enemies. The tongue can cut through a heart like a knife. It can cause someone to commit suicide. It can bring joy and it can bring pain. It can bring destruction and it can build a bond. The tongue is a powerful tool, use it wisely.

29. Attitudes are contagious. What kind are you spreading?

If you walk into a room with a big smile on your face and speaking to everyone someone's attitude will change. If they were in a bad mood, you will have just lightened their spirits. If you walk into a room with a bad attitude and start snapping at the people around you, those people will change their attitudes and in return be snappy as well. They will give you a hard time. The attitude that you brought into the room spread to everyone else. So you always want to have a positive attitude. If you are always positive and try to do positive things in your life, the people who are watching you will have that same positive attitude because your positive attitude has rubbed off on them.

30. The two most powerful words - 'I'm sorry', could literally save your life.

If you stepped on the feet of a person who is very particular about his brand new shoes and don't say 'I'm sorry' you could be in for a lot of trouble. People have been known to shoot and stab someone for stepping on their shoes. If you say or do the wrong thing to a person and don't say 'I'm sorry' you could be compromising your relationship. Some people will hold grudges or try to hurt you even though you didn't mean to cause any harm. Remember to say I'm sorry when you offend someone. if not, this could lead you to an uncompromising position, especially with the mental state of some people. I'm sorry is a powerful word to use.

31. Choose your battles wisely.

Not every battle is worth fighting. Everything can't always go your way. If no harm is being caused and the struggle is because of the way you think, then you may want to think twice about disturbing the peace. If someone forgot to close the bread, close it up, and do a friendly reminder if necessary. No need to yell. Yes, speak up when something is bothering you because it can cause an explosion after so long, but choose your battles wisely.

32. Remember to say, 'I haven't done it yet', rather than, 'I can't do it'.

When faced with new challenges, don't back away because you haven't done it before. Just because you haven't done it before doesn't mean that you can't do it. Try it and do your best, you may be great at the newly discovered talent.

33. If you fail to plan, you plan to fail.

When you take a road trip, you map out your location and the route that you are going to take. If you were to bake a cake you make sure that you have all the ingredients before you start. If not then you may find yourself having to stop in the middle of making your cake to go to the store to get some of your ingredients. Write out the business plans for your new business so you will have an idea as to what you have to do in order to be successful. Always plan your life and your events to make sure you have everything in order. Changes and detours may occur but at least you won't go in blindsided.

34. Never take anything for granted, your life nor your family and friends.

Always treat your body right. Put the right foods in it. Don't just feed your body junk foods and alcohol. If you take care of your body, your body will take care of you. Never think that you can treat your friends and family any kind of way and they will accept you. They have the option to love you or to leave you hanging. Love and cherish your family and true friends because one day they may not be there for you when you need them. Jobs come and go, don't think that you are indispensable on your job. Always have an option that is in the corner should something happen.

35. Remember to say, 'thank you' and 'I'm sorry'. It could mean the world of a difference to someone.

When someone gives you something, compliment you, or do something to help you out, always say, 'thank you'. Showing gratitude is the best thing you can do for a giver. It will make them happy and make them want to do more for you. When you hurt someone's feelings or do something offensive to someone, remember to say 'I'm sorry'. You don't want to be the cause of someone walking around with a chip on their shoulder and a bad attitude toward you.

36. Give flowers while they live. Don't wait until they are dead to give props.

Oftentimes people have a tendency to love, admire, and appreciate from a distance. They never tell the person how much they admire their work or appreciate their friendship. If someone is doing a good job and you really admire them, let them know while they are living because when they are dead they won't know.   They can't smell the flowers on a grave after they are dead. Therefore, they won't appreciate the flowers that you give. People need to know that they are appreciated while they are alive. Oftentimes they are disappointed because they think nobody cares about them nor appreciates the things that they do. Don't let your appreciation for someone go on the grave Instead of in the grave in their heart where they can cherish it.

37. Quitters never win and winners never quit.

Never give up on a task or goal because it seems too hard. You may be on the verge of winning or completing the task but you will never know if you give up too soon. Quitters never win and winners never quit.

38. Make your player haters your motivators.

There are people out there who will sabotage your motivation to succeed. They will tell you what you can't do and try to encourage you not to move forward with your plans to succeed. Every time they tell you what you can't do, you make it your business to prove them wrong. Whenever they say that you can't do something, you go and do it. You work your butt off to succeed. Proving them wrong because it is in you and you have the power to succeed. Make your player haters your motivators.

39. In order to be a good leader, you must be a good follower.

When you constantly refuse to follow the rules and obey your leaders, you will have people who are watching and they will refuse to obey your rules and follow your direction when you become a leader. So you cannot be a good leader if you are not showing what leadership and following are all about.

40. Being disobedient and not following the rules is often the cause of our lack of success.

If you bake a cake at 425 degrees when the instructions tell you to bake it at 325, the cake will not turn out right. If you do not replace a part in your car as instructed the car will not run properly. If you do not follow up with the court system when you're supposed to, you could go to jail. Following instructions and doing things right is important for success.

41. The storms that we go through are our strengthening tools.

25

You won't understand it when you are going through trials and tribulations, but all of those things will give you strength for tomorrow. The knowledge that you gained can be shared with others to help them out as well as prepare you for whatever the future holds for you.

42. If you take care of your body, your body will take care of you.

Getting plenty of rest, eating fruits and vegetables, and drinking plenty of water plays a valuable part in keeping your body healthy. You will live in your body for the rest of your life. It will serve you well if you take care of it. If you don't exercise and you use an excessive amount of drugs and alcohol your body will weaken. Your kidneys and liver have to filter those toxins out of your body. If you overload your organs they will malfunction and cause you health problems if not kill you.

43. For every action, there is a reaction.

If you are smiling and have a jolly attitude, people around you will start to have a jolly attitude as well. If you are nasty to the waitress, you may be waiting a long time for your food. If you are a liar or a bully you will find yourself not having friends. They will walk away from you. If you stay over and do more than your share of the work on your job you will be noticed and you will get promoted and recognized for your extra efforts. If you draw your fist up to hit someone they may shoot or stab you before you make contact. If you rescue someone from danger you may get national recognition and a nice monetary reward. If you help someone to get up or just to stand on their own two feet, you may not see the reaction immediately but the gratitude will come somewhere down the road.

44. Focus on the solution, not the problem.

If your house was on fire, don't just say "oh my God, oh my God, my house is on fire". Get some water to put it out. Get out of the house safely and call the fire department. If you have a flat tire on your way to work, fix it, and call your job to let them know that you will be late. If your date for a special event decided not to go at the last minute, just find a substitute. Don't sweat over it. Concentrate on the solution, not the problem.

45. When you have a setback, don't step back. Get ready for the comeback.

You owned a restaurant and the plumbing was so bad that you had to close it down for a couple of weeks for the repairs. Don't close it for good. That was only a minor setback. Get ready to come back stronger than ever. Interruptions in a well thought out plan are tools to make it better.

46. Patience is the key to success.

The price is greater when you rush to get something. It

could be monetary, peace of mind, love in relationships, or losing weight. All could be devastating if you don't take your time in achieving them. Rushing causes excessive stress and this is how mistakes are made. Relax and make sure that all is on the right path as you reach for your goals.

47. You can't see where you are going if you keep looking backward.

People who have been in failed relationships take that memory into the next one. They can't see the good in the new person because they keep looking for the bad in them. Give them a chance to make you happy without looking for pitfalls. Just because you didn't pass the certification test the two times that you took it, doesn't mean that you will fail it again. The third time could be a charm. You learn from your history, not live by it. Many people carry so much baggage that it weights them down. Drop the load and move forward to a better future. History is just that----HISTORY.

48. Forgive so that you can heal.

Forgiving is for yourself. As humans, we tend to hold onto the hurt and pain. Every time we see the person that caused the pain, we would get a little emotional. That person may have no idea that she has hurt you and that is the reason that you treat her the way that you do. You are the only one who is hurting and holding grudges. Speak to her and release the pain. Once you forgive, a burden will be lifted from your shoulders. You can then live in peace. Forgetting may take a minute but at least your healing will start and the pain Will gradually disappear.

49. Something that you've done has gained admiration from a person that you least expected.

It could be the way that you spoke your peace without breaking the peace. The way you shop and buy a lot of things without spending a lot of money. It could be the way that you work to reach your goals and not letting anyone stop you. It could be the way you always smile and make people feel good about being around you. You may be the person who gives someone the strength to stand up to domestic abuse just by watching your actions. Never think that you are in this world alone and no one is paying attention to you. They are noticing but you may never know.

50. Your personality can literally change a person's life.

If you are one of those Happy-Go-Lucky people, always smiling, always complimenting someone, and just being nice, you could be making a huge difference in someone's life. At home all they may hear is "you're ugly" and "you will never amount to anything". Your kindness may prevent them from committing suicide or just lift their self-esteem. Your liking politics and wanting to make a change may encourage someone to run for a political office. On the other hand, if you are a bully and always picking on someone, you may drive them to pick up a gun and start shooting people. A person may see you always hustling trying to make a dollar and decides to go to trade school to learn some new skills. You make a difference in a person's life whether you want to or not.

51. Just because you fall doesn't mean that you have failed. Just because you lost a round or 2 doesn't mean that you've lost the battle and can't win. Get up and continue to give it your best shot.

Life is like learning to ride a bicycle. At first, you are all over the place. Not only do you fall a few times but you would also run into things and people because you didn't know how to stop and control it. With each incident, you would mount upon that bike and try it again until you have perfected riding a bicycle. You will have to turn a deaf ear to those who will point a finger and tell you to give up, just like you did when you were told to 'get off that bike before you hurt someone'. You have to be just as determined to succeed in your endeavors as you were in learning to ride that bike.

52. There are consequences for everything that you do, be it good or bad.

There is this old saying that 'you have to reap what you sow'. The seeds that you plant could bring you joy or it could bring you pain. And it will come back in 4 folds. If you mistreat your family they will not be there for you in a time of need. If you help someone with a problem, down the line somewhere someone will solve your problem. If you cheat and stress out your employees, their children may bully your child in school or in the community. One tomato seed will make one plant. But that one plant will yield many tomatoes. If you pull them off and share them they will continue to bear fruit. If you let them stay on the vine because you can't eat them all, they will rot and the vine will stop bearing.

53. Never love anybody or anything more than you love yourself.

We often put other people's wants and needs in front of ours. We will sacrifice our bill money to give to someone else and they won't give it back. You spend your time with your friend when you really want to and need to take care of your business. Then when you ask for help you are turned down. Love yourself and take care of your needs before you take care of anyone else's needs. Don't go to work sick because you feel that they need you. Your life and health are more important. If push comes to a shove, they will replace you without thinking twice about it. Never ever let yourself suffer for the sake of pleasing someone else. Love yourself more.

54. Never let anyone else control your destiny.

If your heart is to go into the medical field and become a nurse, don't let someone talk you into computer programming. When your only desire for a computer is to get your email and to do some occasional research, you will be very unhappy in changing. Whereas your helping and taking care of the sick feels very rewarding. If you make a mistake in your chosen destination, let it be your mistake, not someone else's.

55. Always believe in yourself whether anyone else does or not.

If your greatest desire is to become a movie star, go for it. Never let anyone tell you to come out of that dream world and get a real job. Dreams become reality with hard work. It is your dream and desire, not theirs. Therefore, they won't have the same faith as you have in this venture. Remember you control your destiny, not anyone else.

56. Your actions speak louder than your words.

Just saying "I Love You" doesn't mean as much as a sandwich when you are hungry, a phone call to check up on you, an ear when you need someone to listen, a ride when you are stranded, a joke when you are sad or a travel buddy when you go somewhere. Those are actions of love. Those little things mean so much. Baking a delicious cake speaks louder than bragging about your skills to bake one. Change the light bulb if you said that you can and will. If you don't, your word can't be trusted. Working hard to accomplish something speaks louder than just saying that you want to do it.

57. People learn by example. What examples are you displaying?

If you are cursing and stealing in front of a child, he will learn to do the same thing. When you come back from break on time and treat your co-workers with dignity and respect, they will do the same thing. Going to school and trying to better yourself will inspire someone else to get an education as well. We are all leaders in some form whether we know it or not. Setting good examples will make you an even greater leader.

58. The smallest thing that you say or do could mean the world to someone else.

Work is over and your co-worker is waiting for her ride to pick her up. He is late and you wait with her until he comes. You see someone making a mistake and you let them know before they get into trouble. You tell someone who has low self-esteem that they are pretty/handsome and that you love their smile. You see a sad face and you ask them to go walking with you to get some ice cream, your treat. All could have been done at a low point in their lives and your act of kindness made a difference.

59. Everything that you do will affect you the rest of your life - your study habits, ethics, money management, your character.......

Your friends will remember how you gave away food when you worked at a restaurant and will not hire you to work at theirs. Not studying and learning all that you can cause you to miss out on jobs and business opportunities. Being thrifty with your money could afford you the house that you wanted and to be fortunate enough to have funds for emergencies. You were a bully in school as a youngster. Your child is in a life or death situation and you rush her to the hospital. Now your child is in the very hands of the person that you bullied as a child. What is going through your head? Being mean and arrogant will push people away - you won't have many friends. Kind people will always have friends, even when they are far away.

60. Know the difference between a detour and a dead end.

Just because things don't go as you have planned doesn't mean that you have completely failed. You just have to make some changes in your plans. An obstacle may prevent you from having the party at the place that you had planned so you go to another venue. Make the adjustments; don't just stop in your tracks.

61. Goals are met one step at a time.

In order to have a successful business, you must start at the bottom and work your way up to have all the necessary knowledge to run it. The lack of knowledge could cause you to fail. Work in a restaurant to learn all the ins and outs before buying one. Though you may hire people to do many jobs, you will have to have the knowledge to train and lead. You don't become a great athlete overnight, it takes lots of training to get there. How do you eat an elephant? One bite at a time.

62. Every accomplishment starts with a decision to try.

To become a cheerleader you must first try out. No one will know your skills unless you show them. To become a great painter you must pick up the brush and start painting. Hoping and wishing will not get you anywhere. Classes in culinary arts will lead to becoming a great chef. Training and preparation always helps in accomplishing goals. Then you keep going until you have made it to where you want to be.

63. Success is not an accident. It is the result of a well-executed plan.

Success isn't something that you can just buy or jump into. It takes hard work to be successful and to sustain it. You must plan, train, gain knowledge, and execute.

64. Never be afraid to ask for help.

People love to see young people striving to do something positive with their lives. They are always eager to help them to succeed. Oftentimes people have struggles. Be it on the job or in the home, we all need help at one point or another. There are people who are ready and willing to help you if you only ask. They can't read minds. For fear of offending you, some may stand waiting for you to say something. They want to help. Pride may have its place somewhere, but this may not be it. Ask for help, nobody likes to see anyone suffer or make mistakes.

65. Know when to speak and when to be quiet. There is a time for both.

You learn more when you listen than when you are talking. You could tell someone about your business contacts and ideas and they will in turn take it and run with it for their own self-gratification. You could tell someone else and they will tell you that the contact person is bad and will in turn help you reach your business goals. You don't always put your two cents in when you hear someone gossiping about someone unless it is to their defense. Just by listening you will learn their character and discover that you might be the subject of the next group session. Speak up when you see someone's security at stake. When in a heated argument being quiet may save your face or better yet, save your life. Learn when to speak and when to be quiet.

66. Always do your best in everything that you do.

If you are going to be an engineer, be the best engineer that you can be. If you are going to be a bum, you be the best bum there ever was. If you are a friend, be the best friend one could ever have. Be the best mom, the best doctor, the best husband. When searching, one always looks for the best doctor, the best restaurant, the best builder, the best singer, the best repairman, and so on. Always do your best, never half stepping.

67. The only time that you look down on a person is when you are reaching out to pick them up.

Just because you have more money than someone else doesn't mean that you are better than they are. When they honestly work hard for their money, and whereas you may cheat and beat your way to the top, it actually makes them better. Their character makes them likable whereas yours will make you enemies. Be nice to everybody and help the less fortunate when needed without patting yourself on the back. Those may be the same people who may sustain you should you begin to fall from grace.

68. Try to understand why a person did what he did rather than judging him on what he did alone.

If suddenly you were hit in the back unexpectedly, find out why before you decide to retaliate. He may have just killed a bee on your shoulder and you are allergic to bees. A co-worker may become emotional and snappy. When talking to her you may find that she has been keeping late hours with her sick mother and is worried that she may be dying. When a child is asking for your food in the cafeteria, it could be that that is the only food that he has to eat. There is no food at home to eat. Work on understanding before judging.

69. Negative people are dream crushers. Don't share your dreams with them.

Just because people don't have the same dream as

you, they won't believe in yours. They will tell you that it won't happen or that you can't do it. They will have negative things to say to discourage you from reaching for your goals and fulfilling your dreams. They won't be happy for you when you reach a milestone and mock you when you slip. Lift your shoulders, keep your mouth shut and let your light shine.

70. You don't have to put out someone else's light to make yours shine.

Degrading and putting someone down doesn't make you a big person, it's just the opposite. Uplifting and praising actually makes your light shine brighter. There are enough praise and opportunities for everyone. Rise up and shine together.

71. The more players hate, the taller you stand.

There will be people who don't want you to succeed. They will refuse to help you and sometimes sabotage your projects. You will be disliked because you are pretty or because you appear to be intellectual and get along with your peers. Having a side hustle to make ends meet and being supported by the community can cause you to have enemies. The more they hate, the taller you stand. Don't quit or back down to satisfy their egos. They have the problem, not you. Make them come up to your level or continue to live in envy. You don't have to say anything. Just know within yourself that you are going to make it and that you have something that they wish they had,

72. Having CPR will boost your quality of life (Courtesy, Politeness, and Respect)

It pays to be nice - literally. The recognition of your being nice and courteous to your co-workers could mean a promotion and a raise. Being respectful to the elders as well as your peers will earn you respect. Not only will CPR make you liked by the community but it will also open doors for you before you get to it.

73. A setback is an opportunity to improve on your shortcomings.

Things don't always turn out the way that we have planned it. Take the time to analyze what went wrong or what can be better. That's how we learn, be it a relationship or a project. You will learn the telltale signs of a bad relationship so you will know what to look for the next time. On projects, you will add, subtract, or tweak to make it the way that you want it.

74. Don't assume or expect that everyone has the same knowledge and strengths as you.

We all have different talents and knowledge. That's what makes the world go around. A chef may be able to draw circles around you in the kitchen and you may be able to draw circles around someone in computers. People don't even have all the same words in their vocabularies. One person is scared of snakes while another is afraid of roaches. Everyone has their own unique make-up. So don't be shocked when you run across someone who doesn't like chocolate when you have an addiction to it.

75. Never be jealous or compare yourself to others.

What looks good may not be good. A cake may be decorated really pretty, but when you bite into it you may choke. Your cake may not be the best decorated but it sure is mouth-watering good. A person may come to work early and stay late every day. They get the promotion that you were hoping to get. What you don't know is that she spends so much time at work because she doesn't want to face the abuse at home. Every time you see a certain person they are dressed to the T in designer clothes. And you wish you could be like that. Those clothes could have been borrowed or stolen if not from the thrift store. A store appears to be up and popping really well. But what you don't know is that the owner is sleeping in the inventory room and is barely eating. You will never know what some people have to go thru to get to where they are or appear to be.

76. Always have a friend that you can count on and trust.

You can't say that you don't need friends and be telling the truth. You need someone to share your joys with, to share your frustrations with, to give you some advice, to tell you when you are wrong, to go places with and to laugh with. It can be one person whom you can call upon whenever you need to talk to someone, or take you to the hospital or pick you up from the bus stop. Having one friend is good but 2 or 3 is better.

77. Always save for a rainy day.

Never spend all your money as soon as you get it. You always want to have money available in case of an emergency. If you get sick and can't work you will have that money to fall back on. If your car suddenly breaks down, your emergency funds will sustain you. If you see an outfit that you just got to have, the money will be there. Always put a little of each paycheck away for that rainy day.

78. Don't just settle.

Don't settle for just working at McDonald's when you can own a McDonald's franchise. Don't settle for a "C" when you can get an "A". Don't settle for anybody just to be in a relationship. You want a wholesome and healthy relationship. One that makes you feel good to be in. Always strive to reach higher goals.

79. In order to know you and understand who you are, you must know where you came from.

In addition to developing our own identity and personality, we have inherited a lot of our characteristic traits from family members. Be it your smile, your height, your debating attitude, your love for music, your entrepreneurial spirit, and more. These characteristics can come from your grandparents, parents, and even farther back. In doing your research you may find that you got your artistic ability from your great grandfather or your guts to stand up for your rights from your mother. Learn about your family history, medically it could be a lifesaver.

80. Accept a person for who they are and not who you want them to be.

Many people make the mistake in thinking that they can change a person once they are in a relationship. Some personality traits can be intolerable or embarrassing for those who want to be around perfect people. Trying to entice a person to change their personality can put a strain on the relationship. Everybody has quirks that's not appealing to some but loved by others. Accept them for who they are. The difference can be enlightening.

81. Violence isn't the answer.

Violence begets violence and it will only end with someone getting hurt or killed during the process and the problem is still not solved. You should never hit someone because they made you angry. And you should never be used as a punching bag for someone to release their frustrations. So many people have confused love with abuse. Love should never make you jealous enough to strike a person. That's not loving, that's control. Never accept "You made me do it" from a spouse because love doesn't hurt. Love yourself enough to walk away from abuse and respect yourself enough not to strike someone out of anger or control.

82. To truly appreciate the sunshine you must go through the storms and the dark clouds.

You complained about your good paying job until one day you went to work to find that it had burned down during the night. Your rent was due, you had child care expenses, your car note was due and it was time to buy food for the house. And you weren't saving for a rainy day. When it rains it pours. You thought that you had good health. You were always eating junk foods, not exercising, and keeping late hours. Then, during your annual physical you were told that you had cancer. Now you know that you have to take better care of your body. Never take anything for granted -- here today, gone tomorrow.

83. Take pride when someone calls you a geek or nerd.

When someone calls you a geek or nerd they are trying to hurt your feelings. But what they are really doing is saying that you are smart and they know that you are smart. So take pride when they call you a geek or nerd and never do less than your best.

84. It's ok to stand or be alone.

If you are with a group of friends and they want to do

something wrong, it's ok to say no and walk away. I would rather them say "there goes a scared chicken", than "there goes a dead chicken". If they get into trouble, who will have the last laugh? If nobody will go to a movie or a concert with you, it's ok to go by yourself. You may have more fun and be less stressed. Though we love to be accompanied by our friends and loved ones to certain events, it is sometimes better that we go alone.

85. Never give up on your goals and dreams.

I know at times it seems as though you will never achieve your goals and dreams. There are always obstacles in your way. Be it family, finances, education, or illnesses. Never give up on your goals. You may have to stop and rest, but never give up. You may have to change directions, but never give up. You may make some mistakes along the way, but never give up. You may have to ask for help, but never give up. You may have to put it in a corner, but never give up. It may take you 40 years, but never give up. It may be a slow process but you must keep your eyes on the prize. Never let the haters talk you into giving up on your dreams because if in your mind you can conceive, and in your heart, you really do believe that you can achieve, then you shall succeed. The power is yours.

My Choice

I choose whether or not I will get angry today.

I choose who I want for my friends.

It is my choice to have a positive attitude where ever I go.

I choose to be happy and drug free. You can't make that choice for me, I won't let you.

I am in control of my life, my happiness, my destiny.

My mind is elevated and I have the power to conceive, achieve, and succeed.

Attitude is everything, and I can make things happen because it is my choice.

My Empowerment Affirmation

On this date _____ I affirm that I will:

....

....

....

....

....

....

....

....

....

....

....

....

....

....

....

....

....

....

....

....

....

....

....

....

....
....
....
....
....
....
....
....
....
....
....
....
....
....
....
....
....
....
....
....
....
....

Signature ....